*To Ronnie the
Hat
Read & Enjoy!
Love
Susannah
xx*

Susannah Davies

A Starful
of Poems

W0007760

BARKER ❷ JULES

BARKER ❸ JULES®

A STARFUL OF POEMS

ISBN | : 978-1-64789-645-4
eBook ISBN | : 978-1-64789-646-1

Barker & Jules Books™, Barker & Jules™ and their affiliates are an imprint of BARKER & JULES, LLC.

BARKER & JULES, LLC
2248 Meridian Blvd. Ste. H, Minden, NV 89423
barkerandjules.com

I dedicate this book to Joseph Crawford, a special star in my life and to all the other dazzling people who have been a galaxy aglow...

Xx

Index

☆☆☆☆☆

John Wayne

A Quiet Man, tall and tough
An American Cowboy, rugged and rough
A swaggering voice, "Get off your horse!"
A Western Megastar, the Duke, of course!
A great, golden, glowing flame
They'll always be, only one
John Wayne

Macaulay Culkin

Was there ever a boy
As cute as a button or pin,
As the adorable megastar
Macaulay Culkin?

I couldn't imagine Christmas
Without eating a turkey bone
I couldn't imagine Christmas
Without Home Alone

George Michael

Oh George Michael, as I write your epigram
I remember the life and fun of Wham
Jitterbug, Freedom and always a Bad Boy
Last Christmas, still gives me tears of joy
But the tears are now of sadness and great pain
Because you're never gonna dance again.

Sylvester Stallone

I love Rambo
With his headband and his gun
I love Rocky
With his black eyes, Yo Adrian!
The unique slurred voice,
The ripped body hard as stone
I love Sly, Sylvester Stallone

George Clooney

One night as I was dreaming, I dreamt that I was sent
To heaven to find, the most handsome gent
I saw a bronzed Adonis and a hairy Samson too
A muscly Hercules, to name but a few
But then I found him, under the Celestial Moony
It was the gorgeous god, George Clooney!

Hugh Heffner

There was a playboy so crude
Who was definitely not a prude
He liked so much to play
He wore silk pj's all day
Thank goodness he didn't go nude

Tom Jones

There was a singer whose voice was the best
Who had an amazingly hairy chest
His name was Tom
And he was a sex bomb
But he gave me a cardiac arrest!

Julia Roberts

Big red hair
Colossal teeth
Every film
A masterpiece
With Richard Gere
She's so sweet
That Pretty Woman
Walking down the street

George Best

There was a footballer from Belfast
Who liked to get totally smashed
But when he played football
He was King of them all
George, you'll never be surpassed!

Boris Johnson

A fascinating London Mayor
Notorious as a Hooray Henry
Popular and prominent
On his bike legendary

With a shock of snow-white hair
He's earnest and fun
A momentous leader
Prime Minister Boris Johnson

Posh and Becks

I adore Victoria Beckham, her smile-less sulky pout
The only sexy Spice Girl worth talking about
I love her little black dresses and sultry dark hair
If she cannot sing, I don't care!

I adore David Beckham with his golden balls
The football player so handsome and so tall
I love his tattoos and his Armani advert pic
But he is better with Victoria, his posh rock chic!

Judy Garland

There never has been a star so grand
As the glorious Judy Garland
Although troubled, when she sang she did glow
I do hope she's now happy
Somewhere Over the Rainbow

Dolly Parton

Big golden hair as bright as the sun
False eyelashes and an ample bosom
A voice as sweet as honey and candy
A lovely laugh, so fine and dandy
A little cow-girl wondrous and jolly
We will always love you, dazzling Dolly.

Brad Pitt

There was a film star called Brad Pitt
Who was breathtakingly fit
He divorced Jen
And Angie then
Why didn't he marry a Brit?

Marilyn Monroe

Her body was an undulation of hills
Her eyes the sky of blue
Her hair cumulous clouds
She just wanted to be loved by you.

Ed Sheeran

There was a man called Ed
Whose hair was vibrantly red
He sang Perfect to a crowd
And Thinking Aloud
But his songs just won't get out of my head.

Cher

If I had liposuction, a nose job and dyed my hair
Do you think I'd look like enchanting Cher?
If I went to RADA and learnt to act, rant and rage
Could I please be in Moonstruck with Nicholas Cage?
If I had lessons in music, rhythm and rhyme
Could I sing "If I could turn back time"?
If I married an icon who was fabulous and funny
Would my ex-husband also be called Sonny?
No, I'm only dreaming and I think it's utterly unfair
I'll never be as amazing as the incredible Cher!

Dean Martin

Dashing Dean Martin, what a guy!
As Italian as pizza pie!
Part of the Rat Pack, nobody's fool
Smart and sleek, the King of Cool
Singing his song, "Little old wine drinker me"
Made this world so happy!

Madonna

There was a material girl who had the lot
On Holiday she was so hot
She sang True Blue
And Crazy for You
But Like a Virgin, she was not!

Elvis

More handsome than a hundred movie stars
Snaky hips and rock guitars
Curling his lip as girls scream in queues
Dancing in his blue suede shoes
Tight black leather and jet-black hair
All shook up with his teddy bear
A rock and roll king so moody blue
Elvis, it's the wonder of you!

Oprah Winfrey

As rich as Croesus
As humble as pie
A generous hearted angel
In the sky

Not snowy white
Miss Black Tennessee
The world's best show host
Will you talk with me?

Simon Cowell

My hands are sweating and I need a towel
I've just bumped into Simon Cowell
High-waisted trousers and a pearly grin
Sexy eyes and a stubbly chin
An alpha male through and through
A mean and brutal judge too
Although not a singer nor an actor,
I'm sorry to say, he's got the X Factor

Johnny Depp

Oh exquisite Johnny Depp
Is now on the naughty step!

Diana Ross

Diana Ross, Diana Ross! You are supreme
The loveliest singer there has ever been
Baby Love, Come see about me
Your voice is heavenly
You were sent from the angels above
Please don't STOP! In the name of love

Freddie Mercury

Saturn, Venus, the Moon or the Sun
Which planet is the most fun?
Jupiter, Neptune or Mars
Which planet has the brightest stars?
I think it was Freddie Mercury on Earth
The best singer on the Universe

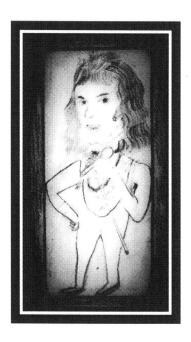

Prince

Purple Rain
Purple Rain
Prince, please sing again
Oh how we terribly miss
Your KISS

Arnold Schwarzenegger

The burly body on that bloke!
He's an awesome Austrian Oak
Mr Olympia brought him fame
And his exceedingly long name
The Terminator was such a ball
Commando and Total Recall
I can't forget his rippling six-pack
And when he says,
"I'll Be Back!!"

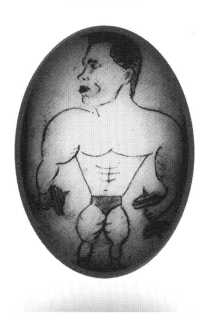

Jon

My brother Jon loves John Lennon, to him he's supreme
His Beatles songs are the cream de la cream!
They both play the guitar and were born in Liverpool
They both love Chuck Berry, they both are cool
John Lennon was a musician who blew the world eternally
But my brother Jon is more special to me!

Catherine Zeta Jones

There was a Welsh darling bud
At all that jazz, she was good
She had beautiful bones
Did Catherine Zeta Jones
But she married Michael Douglas, the stud

Meryl Streep

Mama Mia! Meryl Streep
She makes you laugh
She makes you weep
Thrilling in Kramer versus Kramer
So surreal in Death Becomes Her
The best actress I've ever seen
To you I courtesy, the movie Queen!

Dustin Hoffman

Dustin Hoffman is divine
As effervescent as French wine
Small in stature, a real cutesy
Incredible in a wig
Pure Tootsie!

Neil Diamond

Sweet Neil Diamond
You are so good!
So good! So good! So good!

Tom Cruise

Cocktail was so much fun,
Kelly McGillis and Top Gun
Unforgettable in Rain Man,
Eyes Wide Shut with wife Kidman
Dancing in Tropic Thunder,
Those white undies down under
So good looking and clean cut,
A bit of a Scientology nut
In Mission Impossible,
Simply phenomenal!

Muhammad Ali

So quick-witted
So quick on his toes
So quick to speak
So quick to box foes
He flew like a butterfly
He stung like a bee
He was the Greatest
Muhammad Ali

Frank Sinatra

Like a popping champagne cork
He sang New York! New York!
Wearing a trilby, looking swell
With a voice we knew so well
How the girls would cry
For enchanting Ol' Blue Eyes

Dame Shirley Bassey

From the Welsh Valleys came a black lassie
The oh so beautiful Shirley Bassey
She lustily sang to her adoring masses
With a voice that would break glasses
She sang Goldfinger and Till so dear
But then she broke a Chandelier
She sang Diamonds are Forever quite tender
But then belted out the imitable Big Spender!

Tom Hanks

Who is the very best actor, please say?
Is it Dan Ackroyd or Bill Murray
Laurence Olivier, no thanks!
There would be no Woody without Tom Hanks
In Apollo 13 my heart did thump
And I shed a tear for Forrest Gump
Awwwwww, Sleepless in Seattle with Meg Ryan
Steven Spielberg's Saving Private Ryan
Tom's the best actor without a fail
And my most favourite movie is You've Got Mail

Rod Stewart

A voice like a frog
Too many sprogs
A spiky hedgehog

Drew Barrymore

Her family of stars
In old films I saw
But the loveliest was
Drew Barrymore
A Charlie's Angel
Forever E.T.
A Wedding Singer's love
Pure beauty

Hugh Grant

My beating heart thou doth enchant
Stunning and smart, sexy Hugh Grant

A funeral, four weddings to see
A bad hooker and Liz Hurley

Bridget's diary, for you, top bill
But so gorgeous in Notting Hill!

Audrey Hepburn

A Fair Lady so stylish and sweet, walked over for me to meet
Tall and slender with eyes so clear, radiant like a charming deer.
Hair on top and long black gloves, pearls as white as ivory doves
A black dress with a bare shoulder, an exceedingly long cigarette
holder
She was such a bewitching sight… I could have danced all night
I think I had some epiphanies
It was the star of Breakfast at Tiffany's!!

Goldie Hawn

Oh my! A lady so dizzy
Frothy blonde and so fizzy
Poppy eyes and an infectious grin
A protruding butt and a chirpy chin
A bundle of laughter since the day she was born
The glitzy glorious Goldie Hawn

Daniel O'Donnell

You sing so softly sweet, you are Irish cream
From Donegal to Galway Bay, you reign supreme
A humanitarian with a heart overflowing with joy
I just want to dance with you
Oh Danny Boy

Elton John

The voice, the glasses, the wigs,
The songs, the piano, the gigs
An enchanting star from his hats to his shoes
I guess that's why
They call it the blues.

James Stewart

No man had such a voice
No man had such charm
In Shop Around the Corner
With Margaret Sullivan on his arm
No man could act so movingly
In trouble or in strife
In the Christmas favourite
It's a Wonderful Life!

Bruce Lee

Be like water
Meander free
Be flexible and nimble
Said Bruce Lee
Empty your mind
And please just know
There's no need to fight
If you let life flow

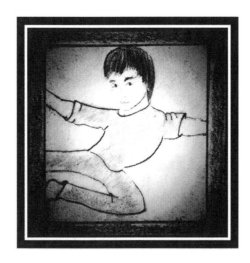

Dwayne Johnson

There was a wrestler called the Rock
Who was tough as a wooden block
He was fast and furious
But it made me curious
He was in bed by seven o'clock!

Harrison Ford

The Hans Solo part he absolutely owns, Star Wars then Indiana Jones
But wow did he magically spark, in Raiders of the Lost Ark!
He should be made a lavish lord
The great, honourable Harrison Ford!

Mick Jagger

Across the stage he would strut and stamp
Looking just a little camp
A body as hot as burning bonfires
Lips as big as tractor tyres

With Brown Sugar he had an attraction
Yet Mick never got no satisfaction
He sang Start Me Up and Wild Horses, wow!
But it's All Over Now.

Beyonce

There was a girl as bonny as a bee
By the name of Beyonce
She had a great hit
Put a ring on it
But now wears a fleece onesie

George Formby

A giggle and a twitter here and there, cleaning windows everywhere
Singing slapstick and cheeky ditties, tuneful songs so very witty
A working-class man, having tea and toast
Always leaning on the lamp-post
Strumming little ukulele to Mr Wu, a funny bucktooth man was you
Grandpa's favourite, it has to be
The garrulous George Formby.

The Bee Gees

I can't imagine a world without the songs from the greatest pop band
Big white teeth, skin tight pants and hairy chests well-tanned

When I hear how deep is your love, how do you mend a broken
heart?
Words and more than a woman, they make me fall apart

Barry, Robin and Maurice, you have given the world disco and jive
I just wish, forever, you brothers would stay alive!

Kelsey Grammer

There was an actor in Cheers
That's been going on for years
He became Frasier
And grew crazier
I laughed till I cried tears!

Elizabeth Taylor

When I was a little girl the first film I did see
Was Elizabeth Taylor in the Courage of Lassie
Then I saw National Velvet and Cleopatra
She starred with her husband Richard Burton, the great actor
Unbelievably big violet eyes that did beguile
No wonder she became a star, with that angelic smile

Rick Tomlinson

I'm pernickety, I'm picky
But I love Liverpool Ricky
Bobby Grant and Jim Royle for years
When Nana died he cried real tears
He makes me laugh, he makes me cry
He is the apple of my eye
So honourable is this man
I'd make him Sir Tomlinson

Jack Nicholson

The crazy eyes, the evil grin
As hot as cigarettes
A villain and a lover
He's as good as it gets
A star in the Shining
But what movie is the best?
It has to be
One flew over the cuckoo's nest!

Leonardo DiCaprio

When he played Jack in Titanic
My poor heart did surely swoon
And when he played ardent Romeo
I saw shimmering stars by the moon
Oh Leonardo Dicaprio,
I love you from your head to your toes
I just want to be Kate Winslet
As your lover Rose!

Barry Manilow

There was a singer who was fantastic
But his big nose was terribly tragic
Then he sang Oh Mandy
And became a dandy
A nose job or could it be magic?

Tony Blair

Do you know what?
It's not fair!
I really liked
Tony Blair
I said, "He's an incredible creature!"
But my husband replied,
"He looks like a geography teacher!"

Jim Carey

What is it about Jim Carey?
His eccentric and super style
That amazing rubbery face
That always makes me laugh and smile
Bad and bewitching in the Mask
Jim, you are the sun in summer
A ludicrous Liar Liar
But forever Dumb and Dumber

Dame Judi Dench

A cut-glass voice, a dignified air
Always charming and debonair
Never a luvvie, a star in the sky
Forever gorgeous as time goes by!

Steve Martin

Steve Martin
Did he ever have dark hair?
Prematurely white
Like a polar bear
But he's sort of cute
That's not doubtful
And extremely funny
As a Dirty Rotten Scoundrel

Ricky Gervais

There was a man called Ricky Gervais
Who had a little fat funny face
The office was great
But as of late
The Golden Globes were a disgrace!

Clint Eastwood

A man as tough as flint
Is cowboy awesome Clint
A Poncho with Pizzazz
A buzz in Alcatraz
OMG to marry
Heart-throb Dirty Harry!

Joan Collins

An ageless beauty who will never walk alone
The stunning glamorous Dame Joan
Always looking dreamy with dresses divine
Full of life like sparkling wine
The star of Dynasty, do you remember Dex?
And all that kissing and sizzling sex
As vibrant as cherries in fizzy gins
The vivacious Miss Joan Collins

Cliff Richard

There was a bachelor boy called Cliff
Who used to have an Elvis quiff
He sang Living Doll
And Summer Hol'
And became splendidly squiff

Kylie Minogue

Kylie was so lucky
Perfect and petite
With a voice
So soft and sweet
As Australian as a bush kangaroo
And always singing
Especially for you

Wills and Harry

What two special Princes! May I say aloud
Tall and charming, Diana would be proud
William with Kate, a beauty by his side
Harry with Meghan, another stunning bride
Although an ocean divides them
And life can be up and down
Their mother's love will always keep them
Bonded to each other and the Crown

Britney Spears

Pigtails and a uniform
I'm afraid it was a crime
That Britney Spears sang
Hit me baby one more time
Because there was a better singer
So perfect for that song
His name was Darius
To him it did belong

Celine Dion

Her voice can be high
Her voice can be low
Clear and powerful
Fast and slow
Singing Immortality
Like radiant rays from the sun
I hope Celine forever
Your heart will go on

Eddy Murphy

In the Nutty Professor
He had so many faces
With Dan Aykroyd
He was Trading Places
As Dr Doolittle
He was so good, please agree!
But he's the best in Shrek
Just as Donkey.

Ben Stiller

Ben Stiller
Always makes me smile
That bemused expression
That beguiling style
He had Something about Mary
And that was shockers
But not as much
As Meet the Fockers

Owen Wilson

Handsome and so fair
Despite his crooked nose
Sexy and smooth
From his head to his toes
In Starsky and Hutch and Wonder
He's got Jewish flavour
But my favourite has to be
Drillbit Taylor

Julie Andrews

In the Sound of Music, the hills were alive
When Julie Andrews did arrive
With a pounding heart so lovely she sings
All about her favourite things
Then with a flying brolly, another movie begins
The magnificent Mary Poppins
She's a spoonful of sugar and never atrocious
She's simply
Supercalifragilisticexpialidocious!

Jennifer Lopez

She can dance
She can rock
Latina Jenny from the block
Her perfect body does impress
In the green Versace dress
And J Lo really can sing
Love don't cost a thing

Princess Diana

I remember your eyes
So beautifully big!
I remember your giggle
Like a merry jig
So tall and elegant
In a shimmering gown
Princess of Hearts
You didn't need a crown!

Ryan Reynolds

Have you seen Ryan Reynolds?
Isn't he super cool?
Gorgeous as Van Wilder
Fabulous as Deadpool
But my dreams were shattered
It's not fair!
When he sang in Just Friends,
I Swear

Samuel L. Jackson

Who is the main attraction?
It has to be Samuel L Jackson
Be it Star Wars or Pulp Fiction
This actor causes friction
A great hitman, it must remain
But don't forget
Snakes on a Plane

Sean Connery

Sean Connery was a Scot
With a lovely spoken lilt
He looked very dashing
In his green tartan kilt
But I have to say
I am much more fond
Of his sexy suits
When he played James Bond

John Travolta

When they talk about the Hollywood Stars, who was the best?
Was it Marlon Brando, James Cagney or Mae West?
They show black and white movies with Cary Grant and Stewart
Granger
Some are as old as the Lone Ranger
Richard Burton and Clark Gable, Steve McQueen and Betty Grable
Burt Lancaster and Yul Brinner,
Tell me please, who'd be the winner?

One Hollywood Star has magic in every single pore
A shimmering shining superstar galore
It can only be the Grease singer and cool dude prancer
The unforgettable Saturday Night Fever dancer
The moves, smile, twinkling eyes and dimple in his chin
If there's a contest for the best Hollywood Star,
Mr Travolta, you would WIN!

Printed in Poland
by Amazon Fulfillment
Poland Sp. z o.o., Wrocław

88808545R00054